Pebble®

# I Am
# Respectful

by Melissa Higgins

Consulting Editor: Gail Saunders-Smith, PhD

Content Consultant: Susan M. Swearer, PhD
Professor of School Psychology and Licensed
Psychologist; Co-Director, Bullying Research Network
University of Nebraska–Lincoln

CAPSTONE PRESS
a capstone imprint

Pebble Books are published by Capstone Press,
1710 Roe Crest Drive, North Mankato, Minnesota 56003
www.capstonepub.com

Copyright © 2014 by Capstone Press, a Capstone imprint. All rights reserved.
No part of this publication may be reproduced in whole or in part, or stored
in a retrieval system, or transmitted in any form or by any means, electronic,
mechanical, photocopying, recording, or otherwise, without written permission
of the publisher.

**Library of Congress Cataloging-in-Publication Data**
Higgins, Melissa, 1953–
I am respectful / by Melissa Higgins.
pages cm.—(Pebble books. I don't bully)
Summary: "Simple text and full color photographs describe how to be respectful,
not a bully"—Provided by publisher.
Includes bibliographical references and index.
Audience: Age 5–8.
Audience: K to grade 3.
ISBN 978-1-4765-4067-2 (library binding)
ISBN 978-1-4765-5171-5 (paperback)
ISBN 978-1-4765-6036-6 (ebook pdf)
1. Respect—Juvenile literature. I. Title.
BJ1533.R4H54 2015
179'.9—dc23                                           2013029994

## Note to Parents and Teachers

The I Don't Bully set supports national curriculum standards
for social studies related to people and cultures. This book
describes being respectful. The images support early readers
in understanding the text. The repetition of words and
phrases helps early readers learn new words. This book also
introduces early readers to subject-specific vocabulary words,
which are defined in the Glossary section. Early readers may
need assistance to read some words and to use the Table of
Contents, Glossary, Read More, Internet Sites, and Index
sections of the book.

# Table of Contents

# I Am Polite

I treat people
with kindness.
I'm respectful.
I don't bully!

**BRAIN TEASER!**

I'm a good listener.
Kids who bully
don't care what
others have to say.

I'm courteous and respect people's space. Kids who bully hit and shove to get their way.

I use good manners when I speak. Kids who bully hurt people's feelings with rude words and gestures.

# I Like Differences

I like all kinds of people. Kids who bully tease people who don't look like they do.

I like learning about other beliefs. Kids who bully make fun of people with different beliefs.

Respect your
classmate's artwork.

You decide how to
solve the problem

Be kind and use
kind words.

# I Am Calm

I find peaceful ways to let out anger. Kids who bully have tantrums. They don't care who they hurt.

I can disagree without getting angry. Kids who bully yell and fight when they disagree.

# I Think about Others

I treat other people
how I want to be treated.
I never want to be bullied.
So I will never be a bully!

# Glossary

bully—to be mean to someone else over and over again

gesture—a movement that communicates a feeling or an idea

manners—polite behavior; people who use good manners are kind to other people

peaceful—calm

respectful—to treat others in a way that shows respect for them

rude—not polite

tantrum—burst of anger

# Read More

**Joseph, Kurt.** *I Am Respectful.* Kids of Character. New York: Gareth Stevens Pub., 2011.

**Meiners, Cheri J.** *Cool Down and Work Through Anger.* Learning to Get Along. Minneapolis: Free Spirit Pub., 2010.

**Rissman, Rebecca.** *Should Theo Say Thank You?: Being Respectful.* What Would You Do? Chicago: Capstone Heinemann Library, 2013.

# Internet Sites

FactHound offers a safe, fun way to find Internet sites related to this book. All of the sites on FactHound have been researched by our staff.

Here's all you do:

Visit *www.facthound.com*

Type in this code: 9781476540672

Check out projects, games and lots more at
**www.capstonekids.com**

# Index

**Word Count: 148**

**Grade: 1**

**Early-Intervention Level: 13**

**Editorial Credits**

Jeni Wittrock, editor; Juliette Peters, designer; Svetlana Zhurkin, media researcher;
Kathy McColley, production specialist; Sarah Schuette, photo stylist;
Marcy Morin, photo scheduler

**Photo Credits**

Capstone Studio/Karon Dubke